People and Places

by Michael Chinery

CRABTREE

Crabtree Publishing Company

PMB 16A, 350 Fifth Avenue, Suite 3308
New York, NY, 10118

612 Welland Avenue, St. Catharines, Ontario
Canada L2M 5V6

Created by Cherrytree Press
© Evans Brothers Limited 2001

Cataloging in Publication Data
Chinery, Michael
 People and places / by Michael Chinery.
 p.cm. -- (Secrets of the rainforest)
 Includes index.
 ISBN 0-7787-0220-0 (RLB) -- ISBN 0-7787-0230-8 (pbk.)
 1. Rain forest people--Juvenile literature. 2. Rain forest ecology--Juvenile
 literature. 3. Deforestation--Juvenile literature. 1. Title.
 GN394.C48 2001   LC 00-060388
 306'.08'09152--dc21   LC

Co-ordinating Editor: Ellen Rodger
Copy Editor: Lisa Gurusinghe
Proofreader: Mary-Anne Luzba
Designed and produced by
A S Publishing
Editor: Angela Sheehan
Design: Richard Rowan
Artwork: Malcolm Porter
Consultant: Sue Fogden

Printed in Hong Kong by Wing King Tong Co. Ltd

Acknowledgements
Photographs: *BBC Natural History Unit* Cover bottom
& back, 5 top, 6 top, 7, 8/9 top, 9, 10, 11 bottom,
12/13 top, 13 top, 14 bottom, 14/15 bottom, 15
top, 16, 17, 18 bottom, 19, 21 bottom, 22, 23, 24
top, 25 top, 26 top, 27 top right, 28/29 bottom;
Michael Chinery 5 bottom, 8 bottom, 18 top,
22/23 bottom; *Michael & Patricia Fogden* Cover
top, 12 bottom, 21 top, 25 bottom, 26 bottom,
26/27, 27, 28/29 top, 29; *Susan Fogden* 6/7
bottom, 11 top, 20, 20/21; *Nick Gibbons*
4, 24 bottom, 28 bottom left; *David
Harris* 14 top right.

1234567890
Printed in Hong Kong by
Wing King Tong Co. Ltd.
543210

❈ CONTENTS ❈

❂ PEOPLE AND PLACES ❂

As the world's population grows, more and more natural habitats are destroyed to provide land to build homes and farm crops. Rainforests are among the world's last remaining wildernesses. The three main areas of tropical rainforest are in South America, Central and West Africa, and Southeast Asia. These areas are home to about 140 million people. The destruction and settlement of these rainforests means very few of the **indigenous** people who have lived in the forests for centuries, are able to continue their traditional ways of life.

Fifty years ago the forests covered twice as much land as they do today, but large areas of forest have been cut and burned since then. Nearly 346 million square miles (14 million hectares) disappear every year, an area about the size of the country of Greece.

TREES OF LIFE
Rainforests are home to many of the world's tallest trees. There are also thousands of smaller trees, sometimes more than 100 different kinds in a single acre (2.47 hectares) of forest. There is also an incredible array of **herbaceous plants**. Many of these plants grow up the tree trunks or grow on the branches high above the ground. This rich and varied vegetation has an equally rich variety of human and animal life.

▶ The map shows how little *primary*, or virgin, rainforest remains. When small areas of forests are cut down, *secondary* forest can regrow in its place. If too much forest is cut down, the forest has no chance to recover.

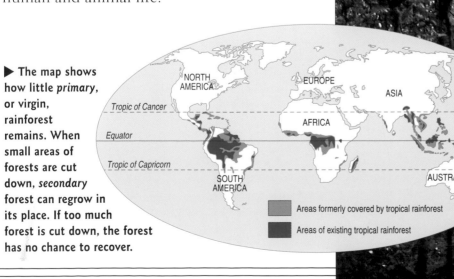

NORTH AMERICA

EUROPE

ASIA

Tropic of Cancer

AFRICA

Equator

Tropic of Capricorn

SOUTH AMERICA

AUSTRALIA

Areas formerly covered by tropical rainforest

Areas of existing tropical rainforest

◄ Trees grow tall and strong in the rainforest. Their hard wood is so good for building and making furniture that many forests have been cut and the trees are now endangered species.

▲ These villagers live in the Congo rainforest in Central Africa. Most of the people farm small plots of land on the edge of the forest. Very few people live in the middle of the forest.

AROUND THE WORLD
• •

RAINFORESTS grow in places with high rainfall. Tropical rainforests grow in a belt around the **equator**, bounded by the tropics of Cancer in the north and Capricorn in the south. In this region the average monthly temperature is above 77°F (25°C). In some of the forests closest to the equator it rains almost every day and over 93 inches (600 cm) of rain falls in a year. In these forests, trees stay green throughout the year.

Forests further from the equator get slightly less rain. Some have dry periods at certain times of the year. These rainforests include the monsoon forests of southern India. The trees are mostly evergreen but some are **deciduous** and drop their leaves in the drier season.

Rainforests do not grow only in the tropics. Some grow in cooler parts of the world, including the northern part of New Zealand and the western part of Tasmania (above). The important thing is that there must be a lot of rain. Plant and animal life in these temperate rainforests is very different from that of the tropical rainforests. Many of the trees are **conifers** and there are also many tree ferns.

⊙ PRECIOUS ENVIRONMENT ⊙

BIOLOGISTS BELIEVE that more than half of the world's plant and animal species live in the tropical rainforests. No other habitat on earth supports such a wide variety of life. The Amazon rainforest is the largest remaining rainforest. It is home to about 3,000 different kinds of birds, over one-third of the world's bird species. More than half of the world's freshwater fish live in the Amazon and its **tributaries**.

Many groups of people live in the rainforests. These indigenous people get all their food and medicines from the plants and animals. The plants also provide them with clothing and building materials. They use the rivers as highways and fishing grounds. Many of them build their homes by the water.

▶ Falling leaves *decompose* quickly in the hot, damp rainforest. *Fungi* and *bacteria* help to break them down and return *nutrients* to the soil.

◄ Villagers build *communal longhouses* along rivers in Southeast Asia. The houses are built entirely from *rattans* and other materials collected from the surrounding forest. The stilts keep them well above the water level.

▲ This Quechua hunter from the Amazon has caught a parakeet with a dart from his blow gun. The bird's bright feathers may be used to make a colorful headdress or other decoration. Nothing is wasted in the forest.

LAYERS OF LIFE

A rainforest has several different habitats, each with its own kinds of plants and animals. The richest habitat is the sun-lit canopy of leafy branches that form the roof of the forest. This canopy is usually about 98 feet (30 meters) above the ground. A number of taller trees, known as **emergents**, push through the canopy. Below the canopy is an understorey made up of mainly small trees that grow well in the shade.

Very little light reaches the ground so few plants can survive on the forest floor. Fungi help the fallen leaves to decay. The trunks of the large trees form yet another habitat. Plants called **epiphytes** grow on them and provide food and shelter for a wide range of insects and other animals.

By the River

Rivers form another important habitat. They are full of animal life, including freshwater dolphins, crocodiles, and hundreds of strange fish. In many areas rivers flood at certain times of the year and the fish spread into the forest, feeding on fruits and seeds that fall into the water. Nearly one-tenth of Amazon trees rely on floods to spread their seeds.

Along river banks, where light does reach the ground, there is a thick tangle of vegetation. Antelopes and other animals live here rather than in the middle of the forest, where most of the foliage they eat is out of their reach.

Destruction and Devastation

In the last 500 years, indigenous rainforest people, animals, and plants have been under threat as people have **encroached** on their territory. Millions of trees are cut down every year to provide timber, and millions more are cleared away for roads, farms, plantations, and settlements. Mining and oil exploration have also destroyed large areas of rainforest in Africa and South America. In some parts of West Africa the only remaining areas of natural rainforest are small fragments that survive on slopes too steep for farming.

WATER OF LIFE

WHEN it rains in the forest, some of the water collects in streams and small ponds, providing fresh water for people and animals. The rest is soaked up by the roots and leaves of the trees and the thirsty plants growing on them. In the heat of the sun, the leaves give off water in the form of vapor. Clouds form and rain falls again, and so the cycle continues day after day. Without the trees, the rain would wash into the rivers and out to the sea. Gradually, the land would dry up and the people would have no fresh water.

◀ Rivers are the highways of the rainforests. Forest fruits and other products are for sale in this floating market in Thailand.

The destruction of the remaining rainforests would have many effects. The forest dwellers would lose their homes and their whole way of life. Many animals and plants would become **extinct**, and with them many potentially valuable medicines and foods. People living around the forests would face devastating floods instead of secure supplies of safe drinking water, and **climate** changes would be felt all over the world.

At last, people are beginning to realize the importance of the rainforests and many organizations and governments are now working hard to prevent their further destruction.

MANGROVE SWAMPS

AROUND many coasts and **estuaries** the tall trees of the rainforest give way to shorter trees called mangroves. These trees grow with their main roots under water. Many have special breathing roots that stick up from the mud. At low tide (right) these are exposed and can take in **oxygen** from the air. Mangrove swamps are important breeding grounds for fish, crabs, and other animals that feed on the debris trapped around the roots. Birds gather to feed on the rich pickings. Many mangrove swamps are now in danger. They are being destroyed by industry and housing development in heavily populated regions and by the establishment of fish farms.

❋ LIVING IN THE FORESTS ❋

LIFE in a rainforest is very different from life in a city, town, or in the country. Before settlers arrived and began to chop down the trees, ways of life in the forests had remained unchanged for thousands of years. People lived in harmony with nature, following the traditional ways of their **ancestors**. Some peoples, especially in the Amazon forest, still live in exactly this way, untouched by the changing world around them. Others have been forced to change.

KNOWLEDGE AND RESPECT

Forest peoples live in small **nomadic** groups or in settled communities. Their traditions and customs ensure that they use the forest without harming it. Even hunters show respect and admiration for the animals they kill. The Ashwa people of Ecuador believe that every animal has some kind of spirit or magical power. For example, the anaconda represents **stealth**, and the jaguar represents bravery. Before hunting, the Ashwa ask these spirits to go with them and bring them success.

▼ Ashwa hunters use *blowpipes* and poison darts to catch fast forest animals. Like most of the Ashwa, this man wears western clothing.

HUNTER-GATHERERS

SOME rainforest peoples, such as the Penan of Borneo and the Pygmies of Africa, are traditionally nomadic hunter-gatherers. They move through the forests and eat whatever they can find. Each family group occupies a territory of perhaps a few square miles, but rarely stays in any one spot for more than three or four days. Everyone is equal in these nomadic groups and there is no ruler or leader. All the food is shared and all the decisions are made by the whole group. These Penan children (right) do not live a nomadic life like their grandparents did. They live with their families in permanent longhouses provided by the government of Borneo. Many of their traditional ways are no longer followed.

Knowledge is handed down from parents to their children. Children learn to respect and admire the forest when they are young. They get to know all the trees. They know which plants to eat and which to use as medicines. The children know exactly when trees will bear fruit, and are taught all the skills for catching fish and other animals for food. Rainforest children do not have schools like ours: the forest is their school. They know much more about the wildlife around them than many scientists do.

◀ The streams provide fresh water for drinking and bathing, and fish to eat. These Kayapo children from Brazil will learn which plants are edible and which are poisonous.

SHIFTING CULTIVATION

Many forest peoples live a "settled" life. They live in larger communities and grow much of their food in small gardens around their homes. They choose an area of forest and clear it by cutting and burning the trees and shrubs, but leave the biggest and most admired trees in place. These forest peoples till the soil and plant cassava, yams, sweet potatoes, corn, bananas, and other crops.

The crops grow well for a few years, but soon all the nutrients in the soil are used up. When the soil loses its **fertility**, the people abandon their garden and leave the forest to regrow. They clear another patch of land nearby. The people return to the original site about 10 years later when the soil has had a chance to recover. This system of shifting cultivation does not do lasting harm to the forest.

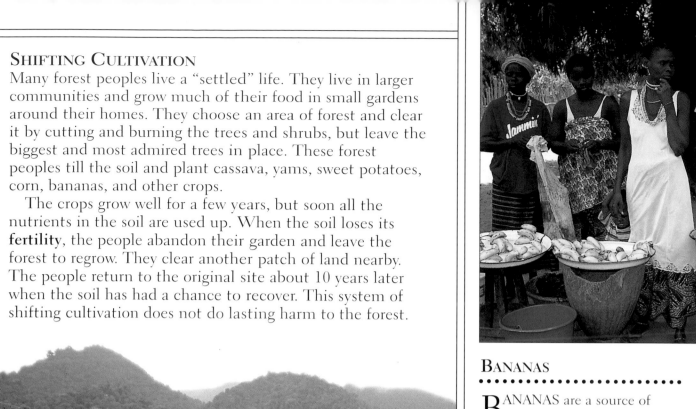

BANANAS

BANANAS are a source of **carbohydrates** and wealth. Big companies purchase entire crops from poor farmers for low prices, or the companies grow

them on **plantations** where they pay low wages. They sell the bananas around the world for a large profit. These women from Senegal in Africa (above) grow enough to feed their families and sell the rest by the roadside.

▲ Animals in the forest are at constant risk from *poachers*. This park warden in the Virunga National Park in central Africa, is removing a snare set to catch antelopes. The poachers can sell the skins, the meat, and the horns.

HAMBURGERS
• • • • • • • • • • • • • • • • • • •

HAMBURGERS and beef products are popular foods in North America but grazing land and labor are expensive. It is cheaper to clear rainforest land for **pasture** (left) in Central and South America. Rainforest soils are so poor, that the pasture does not last long. Within ten years the cattle will have eaten all the thinning grass, leaving the exhausted soil exposed. With no trees left to provide seeds, there is no way that the forest can grow again. Even if there were seeds, the soil is too poor for them to take root and grow. Eventually, the wind blows away the soil, leaving bare rock on land that was once thriving rainforest.

BATTLE FOR SURVIVAL
Most indigenous rainforest people have had contact with the outside world. A continuous stream of loggers, road-builders, miners, rubber planters, ranchers, scientists, and **missionaries** have made their way into the forests, often with disastrous results for the indigenous peoples. Many have seen their homes and homelands disappear altogether.

Governments have resettled indigenous people in camps often far from their original homes. To live, they have no choice but to work for the logging and mining companies or on the huge cattle ranches.

Many indigenous people have no **immunity** to diseases such as measles and influenza which people from the outside world carry. These common diseases kill many indigenous people. During the last century, as many as 90 groups of **Amerindian** peoples with different cultures, languages, and traditions died in Brazil. Many more indigenous rainforest peoples will die if they are not allowed to continue their traditional ways in undisturbed forests.

❂ PEOPLES OF THE AMAZON ❂

THE AMAZON rainforest covers an area of more than 1,235 million acres (500 million hectares.) Hundreds of different peoples once lived in the forest, each with their own language and customs. Today, only about 100 groups, or 300,000 people survive. Forest cultures are disappearing as the indigenous peoples come into contact with settlers and adopt their ways. Many now wear clothing, tools, and weapons that are made in factories. These people are experts in forest management, but are now outnumbered by settlers who are destroying the rainforests.

YANOMAMI

The Yanomami are the largest group of Amazon people still following a traditional lifestyle. About 20,000 Yanomami live in protected areas of forest in Brazil and Venezuela. They live in small villages and practice shifting cultivation.

▼ Amazon children learn to respect nature. Although they hunt and eat monkeys, they also love them as pets.

▲ Raw cassava contains poison that has to be removed before it can be eaten. Women soak the chopped tubers and then squeeze the mush dry in tubular baskets. The poison is rinsed away with the water.

▲ The Amazon River is the largest river in the world and it contains many fish. In some places fishermen immerse stems from poisonous plants in the water. The poison drugs the fish and puts them to sleep, so that they are easily caught. The flesh is still safe to eat.

All the people in a Yanomami village usually live in one large longhouse called a *shabono*. The men hunt with blowpipes and bows and arrows and catch fish with arrows, harpoons, and traps. The women grow crops on the land around their shabonos. As well as cassava, corn, sweet potatoes, and paw-paws, the Yanomami grow starchy bananas called plantains, which they cook before eating. Both men and women gather fruit, fungi, and other wild foods from the forest.

The women also grow **medicinal** plants in their gardens and, although they do not need clothing in the hot climate, they grow cotton for making simple loin cloths and ornamental necklaces. They also paint their bodies with plant dyes, not just for decoration but for protection from insect bites.

◄ The easiest way to travel through the forest is by water. These hunters get everything they need from the forest: their clothing, their bows and arrows, and even their canoe.

LOGGERS AND MINERS

Since the 1600s the Yanomami have been under threat from outsiders who want to **exploit** the Amazon's wealth: its trees, its gold, its precious stones, and the land itself. In the last 100 years, loggers, miners, and road-builders have invaded Yanomami areas, enslaving the people or killing those who tried to resist. Many more Yanomami died from pollution and disease. An estimated one-quarter of all Yanomami died. They are not safe today, even though they live on protected reserves. Gold and other metals are worth a lot of money and mining companies continue to exploit the Yanomami lands, especially in Brazil.

KAYAPO

The Kayapo people live around the Xingu River in southern Brazil. They hunt and fish with bows and arrows, and blowpipes, and gather all kinds of fruits and fungi from the forest, but they also grow much of their food. Cassava and corn are their main crops, together with 14 different varieties of banana and many other edible and medicinal plants brought in from the forest. The Kayapo know what sort of plants to grow on each kind of soil and how to find and kill different animals. They use **compost** in their gardens and control pests naturally. For example, they avoid damage by leaf-cutter ants, by bringing in another ant whose smell keeps the leaf-cutters away.

OIL AND THE WAORANI

THE Waorani and other forest peoples of Ecuador, on the western edge of the Amazon River basin, had never seen an outsider until the 1950s. Until that time they had no metal and made do with simple stone tools. They lived mainly by hunting and gathering, and growing crops. The men and boys were tree-climbers, and their forest life made them strong and healthy. But prospectors found oil on their lands and now there are wells and pipelines where the trees once stood. Many Waorani took jobs with the oil companies that destroyed their homes and way of life. Today, only a few hundred Waorani survive. Other people, like this Ashwa family (left), have been uprooted from their homeland along with the trees. The Kofan people of the forest (above) have no cars and no use for oil. Although oil was found on their territory, they do not share in the profits made from it.

SETTLERS FROM THE NORTH

THE indigenous people of Central and
South America are known as Amerindians.
They arrived in several waves from North
America about 15,000 years ago and brought
maize and several other crops with them. They
gradually spread all over South America. Many
took up residence in the rainforests, where each
group settled in a particular area and developed
its own language and culture. This boy is from
the ancient Maya culture of Mexico.

▲ This Kayapo craftsman is working on
another headdress like the one he is
wearing, which is made of bird feathers.

Much of the Kayapo forest homeland has
been destroyed during the last 20 years,
mostly by illegal mining. The Kayapo, who
have a reputation for fierceness, have tried
to defend their lands, but the miners are too
wealthy and too powerful. A greater threat
looms in the shape of
dams being built on the
Xingu River in Brazil to
provide hydroelectricity
for industries and homes
thousands of miles away.
They will cause flooding
of thousands of hectares
of Kayapo land.

◄ Many displaced forest people
have no choice but to work in
mines. The rainforest that once
covered this open-pit tin mine
in Brazil will not regrow when
the tin is exhausted. The land
will be barren.

❂ PEOPLES OF AFRICAN RAINFORESTS ❂

T HE DEMAND for lumber and for agricultural land, has made the once lush rainforests of West Africa virtually disappear during the last few decades. A few upland areas remain in the west-central African country of Cameroon. They are home to many birds that are found nowhere else in the world. In other areas, most of the forest has been cleared. It has been replaced by cocoa and oil palm plantations. The indigenous people now live in settlements or on the outskirts of towns. Some people work on plantations but jobs are scarce. Those without work grow a few **cash crops** for sale in local markets or to tourists.

PYGMIES

The Central African rainforest in the basin of the vast Congo River is home to many indigenous peoples. The best known are Pygmies, but only a few thousand of them remain. They belong to several groups, including the Bambuti, the Baka, and the Efe, and they live almost entirely by hunting and gathering. They use bows and arrows, and nets to catch animals, and also eat insects, such as caterpillars and beetle grubs. The children learn to identify the poisonous insects from the edible ones at an early age.

Honey is also an important food and Pygmy men climb high into the trees to collect it from bees' nests. They are skilled climbers and link the tree-tops together with bridges made from twisted vines or **lianas**.

▲ These West African people try to make money by selling fruit to tourists.

▶ Pygmies are good climbers. This man is climbing down with a leafy basket full of honeycomb.

▼ The decorations on the faces of these Bambuti Pygmies are mainly for ceremonial purposes now, but may originally have helped to camouflage hunters.

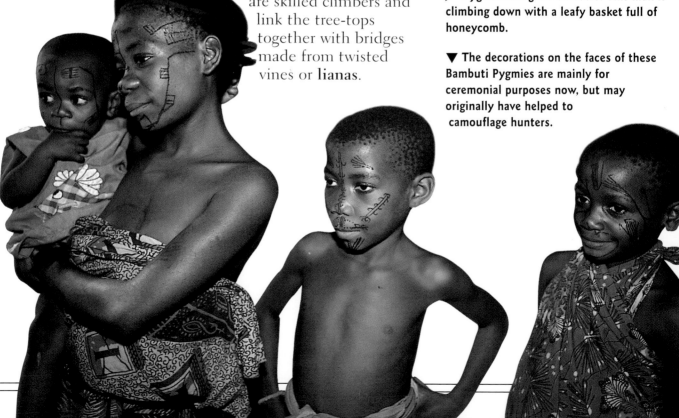

▲ Pygmies make nets from plant fibers and use them for catching animals and carrying loads. They carry heavy items on their heads.

Pygmy people live in small communities of perhaps 20 to 30 households and are always on the move. They build simple shelters with branches and leaves, but rarely stay in any one shelter for more than a few days. They frequently trade with farming communities outside the forest, offering meat, fish, and medicinal herbs in return for cloth, fruit, and tools, such as axes and saws.

SHORT CLIMBERS

The Pygmy people are rarely more than five feet (one-and-a-half meters) tall. Their small size is an **evolutionary response** to thousands of years of forest life. They have adapted to their environment. Small people can climb trees more quickly and easily than larger people. They can also move more quietly through tangled riverside forest.

GREAT AFRICAN APES

CHIMPANZEES (right) are more closely related to humans than any other animal. Chimps live in groups and travel through the shrinking forests of Central Africa in search of food. They are an **endangered species** but are still hunted for food and for sale as pets. The pygmy chimpanzee, or bonobo, and gorillas are especially at risk. Mountain gorillas have become victims of war in Africa and are killed by mines or by soldiers. **Conservation** groups hope the end of war and the end of the sale of animals and animal parts will help chimpanzees and gorillas survive.

❂ PEOPLES OF ASIAN RAINFORESTS ❂

THE FORESTS of Southeast Asia have suffered more from logging than any other area of rainforest. Large areas of rainforest remain only on the islands of Borneo and New Guinea. Numerous groups of indigenous people still follow their traditional hunting and gathering ways in these forests. New Guinea probably has over 300 such peoples, each group with its own language. Some live in such remote areas that they were unknown to outsiders until the 1970s.

THE PENAN OF SARAWAK

The Penan, or Punan, people of Sarawak on the island of Borneo lived as nomadic hunters and gatherers, but most of their forests have now been destroyed by the lumber trade. Less than 7,000 Penan people live today, and only about 300 continue their traditional way of life. These people live in temporary rattan shelters with palm leaf roofs. They live in the Gunung Mulu National Park, where they take sago from palms, feast on ripe mangoes, and hunt wild pigs.

The rest of the Penan have been resettled in camps where, instead of living in individual huts, they share communal longhouses like those of their farmer neighbors. Away from the forest, they have a hard time changing to a life of rice farming.

RICE GROWERS

THE Dayaks and several other peoples in Borneo are farmers known as longhouse people. They live together in shelters (above) that house up to 100 families, each with its own quarters. The shelter is built of poles tied together with rattan. The houses are built on stilts to protect the people from floods and wild animals. The peoples' main crop is rice, and

▼ Sago is the pith of a palm tree. The women chop it, soak it, and tread on it to reduce it to a pulp that dries as flour that can be used in cooking. Rather than harvesting and preparing their own sago, most Penans now buy commercially produced flour.

its **cultivation** is an important part of their life. They perform special rituals during the sowing and growing seasons to ensure a good crop. They also grow fruit and vegetables and medicinal plants in small forest plots. The men and boys hunt in what remains of the forest, and earn money from selling meat and timber.

ENDANGERED APES

ORANGUTANS are among the many animals of Southeast Asia endangered by the destruction of the rainforests. They still survive in Sumatra and Borneo and they are legally protected, but they are being squeezed into smaller areas. Poachers still catch the babies for the pet trade, often killing the mothers to get them. Conservationists try to rescue the captive orangutans and retrain them for life in the forest.

Many Penans now work for the logging companies, but some still go back to the forest to hunt. They bring back meat to eat and sell to loggers or to exchange for clothing.

Although these Penan people survive, their culture is disappearing. The children cannot learn the skills and freedom of forest life, and there are few schools for them to learn about the modern world. The Bateq of Malaysia and the Kubu of Sumatra are also fast disappearing with less than 2,000 people.

HOME IN THE TREES

In the center of the Pacific Ocean island of Papua New Guinea, on the steep forested slopes of the mountains, live several groups of hunter-gatherers who traditionally made their homes high in the trees. They include the Korowai and the Kombai, whose tree houses were as much as 164 feet (50 meters) off the ground. In the past, these homes were more easily defended from enemies than homes on the ground.

Today, there is no need to defend against enemies, and some families are now building homes on the ground. They still hunt animals with bows and arrows, but now their main source of food is sago.

◀ A Penan mother with her baby. His carrier is homemade from bark and rattan, and can be used for carrying other loads. When he grows up, his own children may be carried in a factory-made plastic carrier.

❋ FORESTS UNDER THREAT ❋

DESPITE THE warnings of conservationists and scientists, many of the remaining areas of rainforest are still in danger from the world's expanding human population. Even rainforests in national parks and other protected areas are being destroyed as people move in and cut down the trees. Hundreds of animals are now rare and hundreds more are extinct as their homes were destroyed.

CHANGING LIVES

Many of the rainforest's indigenous people have also disappeared. When Portuguese settlers first arrived in Brazil about 500 years ago there were probably about five million Amerindians in the country, most of whom lived in the rainforest.

▼ A road cuts through the Amazon forest in northern Brazil. Almost all the Nambiquara people died when a road was built through their territory because they had no immunity to the diseases the road workers brought with them.

CUTTING DOWN TREES

LOGS from the Indian rainforest (above) await transport to the timber factory. Timber has always been taken from the rainforests for fuel or for building or making furniture. For a long time the forests were treated like mines, with enormous quantities of timber being taken out and nothing put back – so the forests quickly shrank. Today, conservationists try to ensure that all timber comes from **renewable resources** – either from plantations or from well-managed forests where every tree cut down is replaced with a young one for the future. Unfortunately, not all governments are concerned with conservation.

WARFARE

WARS in Central Africa have affected the people and animals of the rainforests. People uprooted by the fighting have been forced to live off the rainforest land. **Refugees** fleeing from the civil war in Rwanda in the 1990s moved into the neighboring Democratic Republic of Congo and started to cut down the forests for fuel to cook their meals (left) at a rate of hundreds of tons (tonnes) a day. Gorillas in and around Rwanda were also affected by the war. Some gorillas were killed in the fighting and others were driven from their habitats when people moved into the forest. The animals are now protected but it is still difficult to keep them safe from poachers.

Today there are fewer than 300,000 Amerindians left in Brazil. Most of them have abandoned their traditional ways of life and do not live in the rainforest anymore. Forced to leave their rainforest homes because of logging, they now live in camps or settlements set up by governments. Although the governments want them to join with the rest of the population, the people are often unhappy and unable to adapt to their new lives.

The rainforest peoples who do maintain their traditional ways of life have all had their lives changed by contact with the outside world. Many now wear factory-made clothing and shoes, and use guns for hunting instead of blowpipes or bows and arrows.

▼ Many people in Southeast Asia do not have enough food. Rice fields can feed more people than rainforests. People also use wood from the forests for fuel.

▶ This huge dam will provide electricity for the fast-growing cities of Brazil. The people and animals that lived in the area of forest covered by the lake lost their homes.

FROM FOREST TO FARM

The conversion of forest to farmland continues in all rainforest areas. By the 1980s, about a quarter of the Central American rainforest had been turned to cattle pasture to satisfy the demand for cheap beef in the United States. The pastures were generally of poor quality and many have now been abandoned. Much of the land would have been better used to grow crops for local people to eat. Much of West Africa's rainforest has also been replaced by poor-quality farmland or by cocoa and oil palm plantations. The rainforests of Southeast Asia have been replaced by extensive ricefields and by plantations of rubber trees and oil palms.

ROADS TO RUIN

Plantations, mines, and logging companies all need roads to get people and equipment into the forest and their products out. Roads are also necessary to link countries and cities. But roads cause problems. As well as destroying trees and driving people from their homes, they allow newcomers to settle in the forest.

▼ A roadside village in Cameroon, West Africa, where conservationists are working with local farmers to increase the productivity of the land. This will reduce the need to move further into the remaining forest.

MAKING WAY FOR MINES

FROM the air, this gold-mining area in the Brazilian rainforest (left) is an ugly scar. The land may also have been poisoned by mercury, used to separate the gold from other metals. Brazil probably has the world's largest deposits of iron ore under its rainforest, and also has gold deposits that attract large numbers of prospectors and miners. Huge coal deposits lie underneath the rainforests of New Guinea, and there are large reserves of oil in Venezuela, Nigeria, and Ecuador. Mining and drilling for these minerals have already destroyed or **polluted** large areas of rainforest and driven many indigenous people from their homes. It is not just the areas close to the mines or wells that have been destroyed: enormous stretches of forest have been cut down to make way for roads and to provide fuel for smelters and other industrial plants.

RAGING FIRES

FIRE is a fast and cheap way of clearing the forest. Every day, thousands of hectares are deliberately set on fire to clear the debris after the larger trees have been removed. The ash helps to fertilize the soil, although its minerals are soon used up. Uncontrolled fires can burn for a long time and destroy a very large area of forest and its wildlife. This happened in Indonesia in 1997, when the normally short dry season dragged on. Smoke from fires all over the country blotted out the sun for hundreds of miles and caused health and pollution problems in neighboring countries. Parts of the Brazilian rainforest have also been badly damaged by fires. This area (above) has been cleared for cattle ranching.

Some people are forced by governments to move from overcrowded towns. They end up settling on the edges of rainforests. They clear the nearby forest by the **slash-and-burn** method and grow cash crops. Without **fertilizers**, the soil is soon exhausted, so the settlers move further into the forest and start again. They do not understand shifting cultivation and do not recognize the signs of soil exhaustion until it is too late for the forest to recover.

◀ Jaguars once roamed the forests of South and Central America but now their habitat has shrunk. They are hunted for their skins and by farmers who kill them to protect their livestock.

✦ HOPE FOR THE FORESTS ✦

MOST OF THE world's rainforests are in poor countries where neither individuals nor governments have money for conservation. The trees are a resource that they need for building, for fuel, and for export to earn money from abroad. They cannot afford to protect the forests, so people and governments from rich countries must do so. Many countries and organizations give money in return for assurances that the forests will be preserved. They provide money for the management of national parks, for training park rangers, and for scientific studies. Plans for safeguarding the rainforests must involve the indigenous people and make their needs a priority. Forest people can teach conservationists the best way to preserve the forests, because they have preserved them for generations. They may also help scientists find medicines that will be useful to the whole world.

▶ Angry at the invasion and destruction of their homeland, these Quechua people from Ecuador are protesting a new oil development by blocking the road to the development.

A CLOSER LOOK

UNTIL recently the canopy was virtually out of reach to scientists. Only by studying freshly fallen trees or by peering up with binoculars could they get an idea of the richness of life high above their heads. Modern techniques and materials now make it possible to get up into the canopy and examine plant and animal life at close range. Researchers have discovered thousands of new plants and animals, including tiny mice, that live permanently in the tree-tops. As well as looking for species that will benefit the entire world, they study how the plants and animals live and what their needs are. By studying the habits and needs of rainforest species, scientists can evaluate the best ways to protect their habitat. This researcher (left) is holding a baby three-toed sloth.

▼ ▲ To reach the canopy, a researcher first fires a fishing line over a high branch. She uses the line to haul up a stronger line, and then a climbing rope. With feet and hands firmly fixed into ratchet devices, she can "walk" up the rope in complete safety.

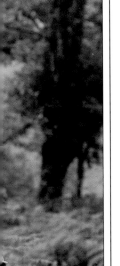

PEOPLE FIRST

All around the world, the peoples of the rainforest have suffered poor treatment from settlers, missionaries, governments, and businesses. Their land has been stolen from them and their way of life has been wiped out. After centuries of poor treatment, forest people are now fighting for their rights to the land they live on. Governments are beginning to take notice of them.

In 1997, the Brazilian government created 22 new reservations for its indigenous peoples, covering an area of over 30,000 square miles (77,694 sq.km), about the size of the state of Maine. Altogether, they have rights to more than one-tenth of the country's territory. The land is not all rainforest and it is not owned by the people, but they have a guaranteed right to live there.

Despite this, their forest homeland is not entirely safe. Illegal mining and logging will always occur because the areas are too big to guard effectively. The people themselves, having seen the financial rewards gained by some of the farmers and miners, also want to exploit the land and mineral reserves. Convincing them that short-term gains will destroy the forest and their homeland forever is a job for scientists and conservationists. Only when the people are persuaded that a better and more profitable living can be obtained from properly managed forests will the rainforests be safe.

▲ Lightweight sectional towers like this one help scientists study the rainforest canopy.

NATIONAL PARKS AND TOURISM

One way for the people of the forests to earn money is to show the forests to outsiders. Tourism generates a large amount of money for conservation and for the local people. It encourages them to look after the forests because they can earn a living and not leave the land. Birdlife International is one organization involved with several rainforest conservation projects. It works with governments to make local people aware of the long-term value of their remaining forests. Conservationists and forest-users are finding ways of using the forest without destroying it. Project workers also help people make the surrounding farmland more productive. This reduces their need to invade the remaining forest.

PACHAMAMA

Young people throughout the world are helping to save the forests because they know that the forests are vital to the world. *Pachamama* is the word for "mother earth" in the language of the ancient Inca people of Peru. The rainforests are the earth's lungs. Without them, earth may wither and die. If you want to help, it is easy to join a conservation organization. You can become involved with interesting projects that will help to save the forests and earth.

▼ **These youngsters are helping scientists to catch and band birds in the forest in Cameroon, West Africa.**

INSECTS GALORE!

BIOLOGISTS study insect life in the canopy by spraying small areas with a mist of quick-acting insecticide, a chemical that kills or knocks insects out. This technique is known as fogging. The affected insects fall onto sheets on the ground below and can be gathered and inspected. Over 1,200 different species of beetles have been collected from the

▼ **Local people can earn money from tourists, who love to buy goods like this pot being painted by a Zapora woman in Ecuador.**

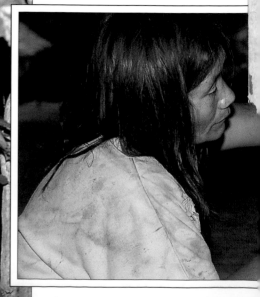

canopy of just one kind of tree
in Panama. Figures like this have
made biologists revise their
estimates of the numbers of
insect species on earth. Instead
of two or three million, some
biologists now think there could
be as many as 15 or even 30
million. The insecticide used
in these studies quickly breaks
down and does no long-term
damage to the forest. This
insect (above) is a bush cricket
from Malaysia.

▶ Tourists admire a waterfall in a
national park in Costa Rica. Too many
tourists could harm the rainforests, so
forest managers limit the numbers.

✦ GLOSSARY ✦

Ancestor A person from whom one is descended.

Amerindian Another name for Native American people, especially those of South America.

Bacteria Microscopic forms of life that exist everywhere in nature and play an important part in the breakdown and recycling of dead plants and animals. Many of them, often known as germs, cause disease in living plants and animals.

Blowpipe A narrow tube, usually some kind of hollow stem, used for firing darts or pellets at prey.

Carbohydrate Any kind of food material consisting of just carbon, hydrogen, and oxygen. Starch and sugar are good examples. Carbohydrates provide energy.

Cash crop A crop grown for sale rather than for home consumption.

Climate Conditions including the temperature, precipitation, and wind that occur in a land area.

Compost A mass of rotted or partly rotten leaves and other vegetation used as fertilizer to encourage the growth of plants.

Communal Shared by the people of a community.

Conifer Any plant that carries its pollen and seeds in cones. Most conifers are large trees and most of them are evergreen.

Conservation The protection of a natural habitat, such as a rainforest, designed to ensure its survival.

Cultivation The growing of crops.

Deciduous tree Any tree that drops all of its leaves for part of the year.

Decompose To decay or rot.

Encroach To take possession of gradually.

Endangered species A group of animals or plants that are in danger of being killed off.

Emergent Any large tree that grows above the rainforest canopy.

Epiphyte Any plant that grows on another, especially on the branches of a tree, but takes no

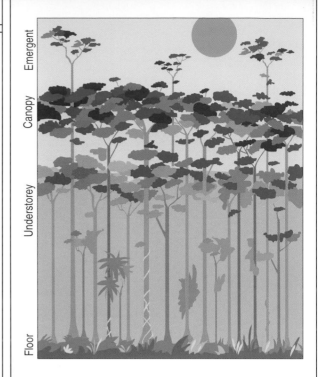

▲ A rainforest has layers of vegetation: low shrubs grow on the forest floor, slender young trees form an understorey below the vast, dense canopy of tree-tops. Taller trees called emergents, poke their heads through the canopy. All the plants are trying to get a share of the sunlight.

food from it. Ferns, orchids and bromeliads are common epiphytes in the rainforests.

Estuary The mouth of a river where it widens out into the sea or mouth of a river where its current meets the sea and merges with the tide.

Equator The imaginary line around the center of the earth, midway between the north and south poles.

Evolutionary response The idea that animals and plants change with the passage of time mainly as a result of nature, so that descendants differ from ancestors.

Exploit To make use of selfishly or unethically.

Extinct An animal or plant species is said to be extinct when it has no living representatives.

Fertility A measure of the soil's ability to support crops or other plants.

Fertilizer Any substance or mixture of materials added to the soil to promote plant growth.

Fungi A group of plant-like organisms that lack

ENDANGERED!

RAINFORESTS are home to more plants and animals than any other habitat on earth. They are important to the world but they are in danger. The people, animals, and plants in this book are under threat. Their homes are being destroyed. If you are interested in learning more about rainforests, you may find these addresses and websites useful.

Friends of the Earth
USA - 1025 Vermont Ave. NW, 3rd floor,
Washington, DC, 20005-6303, USA
Canada - 47 Clarence St., Suite 306,
Ottawa, ON, K1N 9K1, Canada

Rainforest Foundation, U.S.
270 Lafayette St., Suite 1107,
New York, NY, 10012 USA

Rainforest Alliance
65 Bleecker Street, New York
NY, 10012 USA

Rainforest Action Network
221 Pine Street, Suite 500
San Francisco, CA
94104 USA

Greenpeace
USA - 1436 U Street NW
Washington, DC, 20009, USA
Canada - 250 Dundas Street West, Suite 605
Toronto, ON M5T 2Z5, Canada

Rainforest Alliance
http://www.rainforest-alliance.org

Friends of the Earth
http://www.foecanada.org
http://www/foe.org/FOE

Environmental Education Network
http://envirolink.org.enviroed/

Greenpeace
http://greenpeace.org

---

the green pigment chlorophyll and are therefore unable to make their own food. They feed by absorbing nutrients from other living or dead plants or animals. The group includes mushrooms and moulds.

Herbaceous plant Any non-woody plant.

Immunity Not subject to infection from disease.

Indigenous Native to or occurring naturally in a particular area.

Liana A climbing plant with long, woody stems that hang from the trees like ropes. Also known as lianes or vines, lianas belong to many different plant families.

Longhouse Name given to a long building, often on stilts, that houses several or many families.

Mangrove Any of a group of small, evergreen trees with tangled, basket-like roots that grow around tropical coasts.

Nomadic Roaming from place to place, with no fixed home.

Nutrient Any of the essential food materials needed by plants or animals.

Oxygen The air that we breathe.

Plantation An area that has been cleared and planted with cash crops, especially trees or shrubs.

Poachers People who hunt animals illegally.

Pollute To contaminate the air, land or water with harmful substances.

Rattan One of a number of climbing palms whose flexible stems are widely used for building shelters in the rainforest and for making cane furniture.

Refugees People who flea their home in search of refuge in times of war or persecution.

Renewable resource A source of food, fuel or other material that can be renewed regularly by replacing what people remove. Properly managed forests are renewable resources because trees are always planted to replace those that are cut down.

Secondary forest Forest that has developed in areas where the original or primary forest has been destroyed.

Shifting cultivation A system of agriculture in which people cultivate small areas of land for a few years and then move to new areas.

Slash-and-burn A method of clearing the forest by cutting down the trees and then burning them. The ashes help fertilize the soil.

Tributary A stream that flows into a larger stream or other body of water.

Tropics Parts of the world, on each side of the equator, where the climate is hot all year.

✪ INDEX ✪

Page numbers in *italics* refer to
illustrations.